THE
DO'S AND DON'TS
OF EARNING YOUR FIRST
6 FIGURES

A guide for new pharmacists after graduation

By

Dr. Ravin M. Ellis, PharmD, RHIA

Table of Contents

INTRODUCTION

I've been a pharmacist for almost 20 years. As the industry changes along with the salaries, I began to reflect on some of the decisions that I made financially. This book was written with the graduating pharmacist in mind who has the potential to earn six figures in a short amount of time, who may need some financial guidance.

Money management is not something that is discussed very often while in high school or college, unless you specifically take a business class. Looking back over the years, I wish I had known some of the tips included in this book. While I am not a financial genius by any means, my hope is that this book helps someone to see the bigger picture and avoid the mistakes that I made.

I hope that you enjoy this short e-book. It is my sincere hope that this book helps someone to make better choices financially so that they may live their wealthiest life.

STILL IN COLLEGE

Congratulations! The moment you've been waiting for has come! You just crossed the stage and heard your name called with your new title of Doctor. You've worked so hard all these years, and now it's time for you to enter the workforce in the field that you've diligently trained for. The test is scheduled, and your graduate internship or residency is beginning soon. Isn't it exciting? You've sacrificed at least six to eight years of your life to get to this point. So, what's next?

I'm not sure what you thought about upon graduating, but as a wife and mom of a disabled child as well as being pregnant, I thought about the money! Yes, I said it, and I know you're thinking it. Some of you have worked jobs that paid minimum wage just to pay the bills. You have been living check to check, and now it's your time to breathe financially. I understand that completely. I was there. I worked two part-time jobs with a family during my six years in college. I was tired, tired, and more tired. I took out the maximum on student loans during the last four years just to pay some of the basic bills. Well, that was my first mistake, but we'll discuss that later. I just wanted to purchase something without looking at the price tag so closely.

Well, that was a mistake too. The mistake was not the purchase; it was the mindset. After so many years of not having the things I wanted, I began to live as if I had arrived financially. Instead, I should've lived as if I was still in college. It's amazing how quickly money goes when you realize that you have more money that will be deposited in your account every two weeks. Instead of buying the off-brand products that I purchased to make ends meet during college, I began to purchase the name brand products. I didn't cut corners the way I did before. It may not seem like a big deal, but it adds up after a while. Soon, I found myself still living check to check with a much larger income.

The moral to this story is to live like you're still in college. Clip the coupons and cut the corners. Buy the generic brand products. Don't get me wrong. It's okay to treat yourself every once in a while.

However, you must be mindful of those treats. The day will come when you will be able to make that special purchase, knowing that it won't deplete your checking account. However, today is not that day. Stay the course and live well beneath your income. You will reward yourself later when you're not living check to check.

CREATE A BUDGET

Budget. I know. It's the word that none of us want to hear, especially when we've gone without some of the things we have desired over the years. It's the hardest thing to do for some people, but it is necessary if you plan to be financially secure and debt free. I wish someone explained during my college years just how important budgeting would become in my life. Here are a few things that I learned along the way.

First things first. Before you see that first big paycheck, write down all of your monthly expenses. Take the time to sit down and look at every single dollar that you spend. Every penny should be accounted for in some way, shape, form, or fashion. That's the key to budgeting. You must know what you are spending or what you anticipate spending at all times. If you're unsure about a certain category, you may want to re-evaluate that expenditure to determine if it's really a necessity. Remember, the goal is to stick to the budget.

Now, this doesn't mean that enjoying some aspect of your new income is impossible. No one ever said that you can't treat yourself to something nice occasionally. However, the goal is to live as if you had the same income in college for a little while. Doing this will ensure that you will not find yourself living check to check after 10 years of earning that higher salary. If you do decide to splurge for that one time must have, please make sure to plan for that purchase and include it in your budget. Budgets can be adjusted on a monthly basis. Therefore, you can go back to basics the month after that special purchase.

Be intentional and honest with yourself about your goals and your budget. Remember when you had several exams to study for at the same time? You were intentional about your time. You knew exactly how much time you needed to study for certain subjects. You planned that time around your social life and work. You created a plan for yourself to ensure that you were successful in your studies. After all, you knew the anticipated reward for your hard work. Well, look at budgeting in the same manner. It is a goal that you must achieve to live the life that you worked hard for. It is that same diligence and self-control that is necessary when considering your new budget and lifestyle.

EMERGENCY FUNDS

We all know that there are unexpected expenses that come up when adulting. Adulting. That's the word that we use these days to describe the never-ending lists of tasks associated with day to day living after leaving the comfort of our parents' homes. This often means that you are responsible for all of the expenses necessary to maintain the lifestyle you've chosen.

I remember the first time I had an unexpected expense while actually in college. My mother purchased my first car when I was in high school. She gave very explicit instructions after I graduated from high school. She paid for the car in full so that I would not have a car note. However, I was responsible for the care of the car. That meant that I was responsible for the oil changes and maintenance here and there. I'm sure you can imagine the look on my face when

I needed to get a new car after my sophomore year in college due to transmission failure.

My entire world was already different due to the birth of my son. I was managing my expenses, but I was not prepared for a car note. In addition, I did not have anything saved up to help with that unexpected expense. I was living check to check while in school. I did the best that I could considering the situation, but a savings account would have helped to soften the blow. This trend continued even after graduation. I managed to save a little, but that would often be used sooner rather than later. This was an ongoing cycle that seemed to never end.

So, what should you do? Well, I learned my lesson regarding saving money. The first lesson was to open a savings account. You would be surprised by the amount of people who do not take the time to simply open a savings account. If fees are a concern, most banks don't charge a monthly fee if you have a direct deposit checking account with them. In addition, setting up a direct deposit from your payroll check to savings is also an option.

The next lesson was to keep my savings at a distance. While having a savings account at the same bank may save additional monthly fees, the easy access of that savings account may cause you to use the same money you're trying to save. Consider opening a savings account at a different bank that you don't frequent or see often. The temptation to transfer money to your checking just because you know that the money is there can be strong. There are various online banks that offer higher interest rates so that your money is growing while it is sitting.

The moral of the story is to open a savings account as soon as possible and to actually save the money. Emergency funds are a necessary part of life that can save you mental anguish and stress. It may seem like it's impossible at the beginning, but I assure you that saving your money is a discipline that you will thank yourself for in the future.

THE GRACE PERIOD

You may be wondering about the title of this chapter. The grace period is one that most people look forward to after graduation. It can take on several different meanings. It is the time during the transition from being a student to becoming a fully licensed pharmacist. It is the time that students transition from dependent to independent adults. Most of us know this term to be associated with the time after graduation without student loan payments. At least, that's the phrase I remembered most.

So, graduation was upon me. I remember receiving letters from the Department of Education indicating the amount that I would have to pay in exactly 6 months. I remember all the questions that went through my head. "How can I afford these payments?" "Which repayment plan should I choose?" "Should I choose the standard 10 years or the extended 30 years?" I also remember thinking that I would never finish paying my loans off. Well, I panicked and worried about the loans so much that I chose the extended 30-year plan. After all, I had a family, including a special needs son, and we needed all the extra income we could get. I justified my decision in so many ways.

Don't get me wrong. Each person's financial situation is different from the next. However, if I could do all over again, I would have chosen the standard 10-year plan and started making payments during the grace period. Why? Well, most of a student loan is interest. It continues to grow each day. What starts off as a $65,000 principal loan can easily become a $100,000 after interest if you consider paying it off in 30 years. Let's face it. We know that these loans have to be paid off. It is the one loan that you can't get out of, even when filing for bankruptcy. It is the one loan that literally follows you until your death.

Now that you understand that this loan can stand the test of time better than some relationships, think of ways to separate yourself from that loan. I can think of so much more that could be done with that money. So, don't lock yourself into a long-term relationship with your student loan company. Start paying that loan back with the first full-time check you receive. You already know the payment amounts. Even if you don't know the amount or have the full amount, send what you can. Every little bit helps to decrease the interest by making payments as soon as possible.

DO NOT DEFER

We've talked about paying your student loans as soon as you possibly can. However, life can throw you curveballs. As I previously stated, I graduated while pregnant with my second child. I was married and already had a son with special needs. During those six years of college, money was very tight. I can remember the times when I used the credit card just to buy groceries. Once I graduated, things improved some for a little while but not enough. My husband, at the time, was earning a nice salary working for one of the local Louisiana plants. After I was licensed, I thought that things would be smooth sailing. Well, I was wrong. Life happened, and our 2-income family became one income soon after being licensed.

Here's where I made a mistake. Instead of adjusting our budget to a temporary loss of income and keeping up with my student loan payments, I deferred my student loan by one year. At this point, the balance on my loan increased due to interest that accrued daily during the deferment. They say that hindsight is 20/20. As I think back on the situation, we could have managed without the deferment. I could have made smaller payments or made some type of payment arrangement of interest only. There were several options, but deferment should not have been one of them.

While I know that there are circumstances such as job loss or unexpected medical expenses that could lead one to choose deferment, this option should be a last resort. It should not be an option to make you comfortable. After all, you endured being uncomfortable for 6 years. A little while longer wouldn't hurt at all. Think of the satisfaction you'll have after paying off your student loan. You will then have that extra money available to live the life you truly desire. So, take my advice. Do not defer!

JUST SAY NO!

I know. You've worked so hard all these years. The last thing you want to hear is someone say no. You're finally out of school and earning your dream salary. You finally have a salary that will allow you to live and breathe just a little more. This salary allows you to really live like you haven't lived in a long time. So, you finally get that first check. Woohoo! You're excited because it's the most amount of money to hit your bank account since your student loan refunds. You immediately think about how much money you'll have left after paying bills. You haven't quite done a budget, but you tally estimates in your head. Then it hits you! You realize that you have enough money to cover a new car!

Stop right there! Don't do it! Just say no! It may sound like I'm overreacting just a little. However, let me assure you that this is not the time to venture out into purchasing a new car. Now, there are circumstances that may come about that would warrant a car purchase. However, a new car with a brand-new car note after beginning your new career is not the way to go. The emphasis in the previous statement is NEW.

When I was in college, the car that my mother gifted me in high school didn't last as long as I expected. So, I found myself searching for another car in my third year of college. I was given advice from others and eventually purchased a used car that was almost like new. It had 21,000 miles on it even though it was several years old. I was blessed to find a car that was previously owned by an older lady who barely drove it. However, my gently used Honda Accord still came with a substantial car note for a 20-year-old college student with a family and expenses. Because I was so young, my credit was not quite established yet, and it reflected in a double-digit interest rate. The choice I made to purchase this car was not the worse decision, but I could have purchased a car without a car note. This would be my suggestion to you if the purchase of a car is absolutely necessary.

I was once told that having a brand-new car with a maintenance plan and a car note is better than having a paid off used car that needed repairs from time to time. I look back on that advice now. I can now see that fallacy in that statement and the importance of saving money for unexpected expenses. We all know that cars require maintenance. Even the new ones require services every 5000 miles. The key is to purchase a car for your needs, not your wants, and save money for anticipated repairs. Until you completely debt-free and able to purchase that brand-new car with cash, repeat the process.

Now, let's discuss the house that you have already decorated in your head. You may not want to hear this either, but now is not the time. While buying a house is better than renting an apartment in the long run, you don't want to be house poor either. Take the time to plan your purchase and save for a proper down payment. I'm not talking about the typical 3.5% down payment. With a larger down payment such as 20%, you can look forward to a lower mortgage. Also, consider your current bills in addition to the unexpected expenses of a home. While purchasing a home is definitely a goal for many, don't jump into to home ownership lightly. It's a significant responsibility that most don't consider. In the meantime, get yourself together financially so that when you do purchase or build a home, it will be exactly what you've always wanted with no compromising.

PAY IT DOWN/OFF

Do you remember your freshman year? You stepped on campus with a sense of freedom you never truly had before. I entered college while I was still 17. So, the first year on campus was an entirely new world. Although I was still considered a teenager, I had the ability to make decisions for myself without major parental input or hesitation. Here is the time that I proclaimed myself as an "adult." Little did I know that the choices I made in my new-found freedom would impact the rest of my life. I should've known the impact of some of those decisions, but I wanted to show my parents that I could be independent and succeed in doing so.

Well, life took an unexpected turn during my first semester in college when I became pregnant with my first child. As I moved back home the very next semester, I truly learned what it was to be an adult and the expenses that came with it. Before I knew it, I found myself short of money even while working. So, it would be no surprise when a credit card application came in the mail, that I jumped on the opportunity to lighten the load.

What I didn't realize in that moment is that I was creating a cycle that would take years to end and eventually pay off. Over the years, I found myself applying for credit cards so that I could purchase things that I needed and many things that I did not. It became a cycle that I didn't break until a couple of years ago. That's right; the cycle of multiple unnecessary credit cards did not break until just recently after taking a financial responsibility course at my church. It was then that I realized that I needed to pay off all credit cards so that I might have freedom from the debt that I had been carrying around since entering college.

Those same credit cards that at first gave me a sense of freedom kept me bound and living check to check. My intention of paying off credit cards as I made a purchase became just a thought as I tried to keep up with multiple charges. So, my advice to you would be to simply stay away from credit cards if possible, even now. If you've already done the damage, do your best to pay it off. Put a plan in place to knock out each card. Be strategic and intentional. If you know that you have difficulty in this area, get an accountability partner. This is someone who can help to keep you on track with your payments. This person should be able to tell you the truth without any offense occurring. BE INTENTIONAL. Finally, remember that no one wants to be bound to credit cards, including you.

FAMILY EXPENSES???

O kay. Let's talk about this. You may be wondering about the title of this chapter. Well, earning your first six figures can have many outcomes. One outcome that many don't think about is family. I'm not talking about the family that you are raising with your wife or husband. Taking care of expenses in your own household is expected. However, the day will come when someone in your family will come to you because they need your financial assistance. I'm talking about your mother, father, sisters, brothers, or even cousins.

When you graduate from pharmacy school, everyone knows the potential for the type of income you will earn. Just your new title of doctor alone will draw some to you. You'll begin to see some family members ask you to loan them money. You may even see that you are volunteered to handle certain roles for family functions that are more costly than others. You may even have family members approach you concerning business ventures.

I get it. I understand the desire to help your family. I understand the overwhelming need and want to fix things for close family members. However, when considering the help that you give to others in your family, consider the expenses that you must carry on your own. I'm not advocating that you do not help your family in extreme circumstances. My concern is that you do not overextend yourself and compromise your financial situation.

I always believed that God placed me in a six-figure earning career to help my family financially. I was wrong. I soon became a crutch to some family members who knew they could always call me to bail them out of a situation. I had to learn to say no. You too must be prepared to say no sometimes. Be prepared to be looked upon as mean and selfish when you do say no. Be prepared to stand your ground on the decision you have made. Do not allow anyone to guilt you into giving money that would place you in a situation of living check to check. Remember that you are responsible for you and your family first. Also, remember that it doesn't help anyone progress to financial wealth if we take on the responsibilities of others instead of teaching them to become financially responsible for themselves. Someone has to break the cycle of a poverty mindset.

KEEPING UP WITH THE JONESES

When I was in pharmacy school, I was surrounded by people of all backgrounds and varying circumstances. There were older women who were married and decided to come back to school to change careers. There were younger men and women who were my age experiencing college life for the first time. There were those who were single who decided to become a pharmacist after completing a bachelor's degree. Some came from families who could help them financially, while others depended on their refund checks to simply live.

No matter the background of each student, there's this overwhelming sense of pride that comes over each graduate when hearing their name announced as Doctor of Pharmacy. I remember the feeling of finally arriving when I heard Dr. Ravin M. Coleman (my previous married name). It is that same pride that led me to make some financial mistakes along the way.

My ex-husband and I purchased a home a couple of years after I graduated. It was a beautiful home with 4 bedrooms, 2 and ½ bathrooms, a game room, a media room, and a beautiful staircase. It was a dream home. However, it was an unnecessary home at the time. As I look back on that purchase, I realized that we were trying to keep up with the people who surrounded us, and the title attached to my name. It only seemed right to be a doctor living in a 3300 square foot home built by one of the leading builders in the area. It was what we wanted, but it was definitely not what we needed. We were living in debt with 2 children, one of whom was special needs, trying to prove a point that we had arrived. Knowing what I know now; I would've suggested that we purchased a smaller house with a smaller mortgage until all debt was paid off.

CONCLUSION

I sincerely hope that you enjoyed this book. There are some tips included in this book that will help you avoid the pitfalls of money mismanagement when adjusting to a new and larger income. You've worked extremely hard to become a pharmacist. Now it's time to get debt free so that you may live the life you've always wanted!

Congratulations in advance on becoming a licensed pharmacist and stepping into financial freedom!

I wish you success in all your endeavors, Doctor!

ABOUT THE AUTHOR

Dr. Ravin M. Ellis, PharmD, RHIA, is an experienced pharmacist of almost 20 years who has a passion for helping others achieve their goals in health and wealth by avoiding the financial pitfalls that consume many individuals. Dr. Ravin is the founder of the Kyron D. Coleman Memorial Foundation that assists siblings of specials needs children with scholarships to further their secondary education. She is also the author of the blog, "Kyron's World" where she is passionate about helping families to succeed in life, whether financially or through acts of service. She is the mother of two beautiful children and one beautiful angel who bears the name of the foundation.

If you would like to contact Dr. Ravin M. Ellis, PharmD, RHIA, please email her at drravinpharmd@gmail.com or visit the website at www.drravinpharmd.com.

www.ingramcontent.com/pod-product-compliance
Lightning Source LLC
Chambersburg PA
CBHW071445210326
41597CB00020B/3942